CAREER MAPPING
FOR NONPROFITS

CAREER MAPPING

MAPPING

FOR
Nonprofits

The Nonprofit Leader's Guide to Attracting,
Hiring and Retaining Top Talent

Nurys Harrigan Pedersen

NEW YORK

LONDON • NASHVILLE • MELBOURNE • VANCOUVER

CAREER MAPPING FOR NONPROFITS

The Nonprofits Leader's Guide to Attracting, Hiring and Retaining Top Talent

Published in New York, New York, by Morgan James Publishing in partnership with Difference Press

ISBN 9781642792430 paperback
ISBN 9781642792447 eBook
Library of Congress Control Number: 2018910334

Cover & Interior Design by:
Christopher Kirk
www.GFSstudio.com

Morgan James is a proud partner of Habitat for Humanity Peninsula and Greater Williamsburg. Partners in building since 2006.

Get involved today! Visit
MorganJamesPublishing.com/giving-back

To all nonprofit leaders that thrive to create a transforming work environment.

TABLE OF CONTENTS

INTRODUCTION:

WHAT IS YOUR LEGACY?

I t is wonderful to see so many dedicated professionals who want to be of service in the nonprofit sector. These individuals are driven by their desire to make a difference in the lives of others through their nonprofit's mission and services. As the nonprofit sector expands, the work environment is growing more complex. I've seen ample evidence that points to this sea change over the past two decades. Economic shifts, budget cuts, technological advances, and, in states such as Illinois, political strife negatively impacting the release of government funds, have made it necessary for nonprofits to adjust rapidly in order to maintain successful delivery of their services.

Now more than ever it has become increasingly evident that nonprofit leaders must focus on putting together dynamic teams that drive the organization's goals with enthusiasm and heart. Having a committed team that is loyal and determined is essential to the over-all wellness of an organization. Nonprofits must also take care to stay ahead of trends in programming and service deliverables in their respective fields and adapt processes to ensure that their social platforms flourish unfettered by delays or interruptions.

The nonprofit leaders I've spoken with all have one common complaint: They are constantly looking for innovative staffing solutions to improve their recruiting processes. I decided to lean in and pay special attention to their biggest concern and quite possibly regret – they lack the time and resources to attract, hire, and retain top talent. After 20 years in recruiting I've had the privilege of witnessing best practices that separate successful recruiting from failed recruiting.

My first book, *Make Your Mark: The Smart Nonprofit Professional's Guide to Career Mapping*, was written to address the sector's need to attract and retain nonprofit professionals who are equipped with the tools necessary to thrive in the nonprofit sector. It is rewarding to see career-minded individuals utilizing the process I describe in the book to improve their professional lives. In it, I encourage employees and job seekers to take control of their professional destiny and enjoy their journey. I tell them to show up as their authentic selves, confident and altruistic. After seeing how successful the practice is for employees, now it's time to share strategies for the employer.

I wrote this book to facilitate the connection between nonprofit employer and employee and offer a solution that makes the hiring process practical, easy, sustainable and effective. Attracting, hiring, and retaining team members throughout the organization should be a seamless process. It shouldn't be confusing, burdensome, or time consuming. This book will show you how even the simplest changes and tweaks to your processes and protocols can yield lasting benefits to your organization. And the best part is, you get to go back to doing what you love and contributing your unique gifts to advancing your organization's mission.

Best of luck on your journey!

CHAPTER 1:

RECRUITING – THE NECESSARY EVIL

You are executive director of a nonprofit with a $2 million budget. Unfortunately, the job you were hired to do is no longer how you are spending most of your time. You are now devoting a great deal of it to helping your managers put teams together and choose the right team members. That's right, you're walking the recruiting beat! And every few weeks, it seems, there is a position that needs filling due to a termination or a resignation you didn't see coming. More than one employee is being affected by this turnover and more than one person's time is being sucked up trying to recruit and identify a qualified person to fill the position. But the person you're most worried about right now is you – your own sanity and capacity. You're overwhelmed with projects that require your attention and tasks that only you can do. The work isn't getting done and you're behind schedule, and a key position that's open is the culprit. Everything is slowing down, including the speed at which you and your managers are able to deliver services and advance the mission of your nonprofit. You are working late and see no remedy anytime soon. You fill one position and another one opens. You are able to hire temporary help or spread the workload among other staff members, but they're starting to grow resentful. You know in your heart that the tourniquet approach you've been using to stop the bleeding is neither practical nor sustainable. It seems that you spend your days putting out fires and agonizing over the vacancy or vacancies, helping manage the workload and minimally keeping up with the work.

Eventually, you grow concerned that you will be perceived by members of your board of directors as an ineffective leader. Meanwhile, everyone is looking to you for ideas about who to recruit and where from, and how to keep current staff members happy and engaged. At this point, no one can be sure of who is going to stay or for how long. Your managers are afraid of making the wrong hire, but equally concerned about having incomplete projects and losing valued team members to burnout. A recruitment strategy driven by scarcity and fear is no strategy at all. Finally, you think to yourself: "I can't afford to spend another day offering support and guidance on staffing matters to team leaders and managers. This isn't what I was hired to do. I need a solution today!"

One of the biggest complaints I've received from clients throughout my more than 20 years recruiting for the nonprofit sector is the amount of time it takes to recruit qualified candidates. Whether or not you have a human resources department to back you up, as a nonprofit leader you are still expected to offer solutions. Heck, you expect this of yourself! You've been in this predicament more than once, or find yourself caught in a recurrent cycle. If you're like me you start to wonder, "When will I be able to get back to focusing on my core mission? Will the time ever come when I am no longer being counted upon to provide staffing solutions?"

Staffing challenges, whether they are caused by high turnover due to mis-hires or poorly articulated job descriptions, affect the day-to-day operations of your organization and impede the successful advancement of its mission. They can also stifle individual contributions from staff members and negatively impact morale. You also worry that the organization may be earning a poor reputation due to its high turnover rate. You believe the work that you do is making a difference, and you have staff members with a long history with the organization who are contributing at a high level to thank for that. Where do you find more people like them? You don't expect a lifelong commitment. But you do expect individuals who are excited about the opportunity and who want to make a difference. No surprises, please! Believe me, I understand, it's no fun coming to the decision that a new hire is not working out after only five months, or receiving a resignation on a Monday morning. Getting blindsided by changes in employee behavior, commitment or enthusiasm is something we all try to avoid.

Of course, as a nonprofit leader you would rather spend those precious hours advancing the mission of the organization. Recruiting is time consuming, I'll give you that, but it is truly a necessary evil. Nobody is spared. Not even a staffing expert like me.

I can recall a time when I was hiring too fast to fill vacancies at my firm or making the wrong hiring decisions, because I didn't want to spend too much time on recruiting and away from my core responsibilities. I just wanted the problem to go away. I allowed the pressure I felt to get back to my responsibilities dictate the amount of time I spent on recruiting, a process that was not very well thought out to begin with due to the time crunch. As a result, I found myself hanging on to employees who were not a good fit just so I could avoid getting back out there on the recruiting trail. Then it happened. I was blindsided by the resignation of a staff member for whom I'd had high hopes. I started to question myself. "Why can't I get this right when I am the expert?"

Ironically, upon comparison, I realized that my clients and I had the same list of grievances:

- Not enough time to recruit
- Not enough qualified candidates
- Surprises, such as unforeseen resignations
- Having to recruit for the same position multiple times
- Having to compromise on some aspects of the role to fill the position
- Managing unrealistic expectations from new hires
- Not having an internal pool to recruit from
- Spending precious hours away from the core mission
- Being forced to get creative with the current work-force to get all of the work done

- Tasked with offering solutions to managers struggling with the same challenges
- Resenting having to wear a "recruiter's" hat too often
- Time and money spent on training and retraining new hires

Again, you just want to get back to focusing on leading your organization and working with your team to advance its mission, as you should. Understanding this frustration has built up a well of compassion in me that I've turned into strategies to help organizations effectively alleviate these problems. It's difficult to think and see clearly when you're in the moment. Sometimes a sense of confusion takes over and you start to question whether you truly need to fill the position. And even if you do fill it, can you say confidently it will be with a dedicated employee who's willing to go the distance? Loyalty is important to the legacy and workforce continuity that you're trying to sustain. Both are critical components of organizational structure, its growth potential, and sustainability. But it's hard to nurture these essential elements in organic fashion if you're constantly being interrupted by employment separations. What are your board members thinking right now? Can they remain confident in your ability to grow the nonprofit and successfully deliver its programs and services while you fight these staffing fires? Or will they perceive you as not firing on all cylinders?

Some positions are simply hard to fill. These are the ones that you, your managers, and HR wind up recruiting for every 9 to 18 months on average. And you have not been able to figure out why some roles have more turnover than others. The following is a checklist of reasons you should consider:

- Is it the team?
- The work in the role?
- The salary allocated to this position?
- The time of year this position has been recruited for or filled?
- Or is it the way the job has been designed?

You've tried compromising, downgrading your list of "must haves" to "nice to haves." You've formed hiring committees and even initiated a complete overhaul of the recruiting process. But none of these strategies have led to the desired results. You are still spinning your wheels and being pulled into the hiring drama.

What is missing in your process? What can be done differently? This should be easy. After all, you have a great job to offer, an opportunity for the right hire to come in and join an amazing team, and a huge difference to make in the world through the work of your nonprofit. Shouldn't job seekers be clamoring at your door to join your team? Shouldn't your current employees have a desire to grow and build their careers within your amazing nonprofit?

So many questions and unknowns. I had the same questions and the same problems at my company in the beginning. There are key challenges that all employers face:

- Attracting the right people
- Maximizing engagement with the existing workforce
- Offering real and structured career growth
- Having a unified team
- Having a clear vision of what you expect out of each role
- Having a team that is fulfilled, happy, and contributing at high levels

Some nonprofit leaders and managers are too willing to accept these challenges as part and parcel to running a nonprofit. Wouldn't it be wonderful if workforce challenges took up less than 10% of your focus and attention?

If your department heads had all the tools they needed to have a recruiting process that was efficient and sustainable?

If things were different, you would be able to get back to your list of projects where you are moving forward the organization's mission. You would be up to date with deadlines and your time would be spent growing a strong team. Days spent wasting precious hours on figuring how to replace staff would be a thing of the past.

Career Mapping

What you need is a sound recruitment plan that standardizes job roles and clearly spells out the expectations and deliverables associated with each role. This is achievable through career mapping. A career map is a tool that empowers nonprofit professionals to best serve and utilize their skills, experience, and unique strengths, to make their mark in the world. This tool simplifies their professional path with Clarity, Purpose, Direction, and Intention.

Getting you back to doing the things that you were hired to do and the things that you would rather spend most of your time and effort on should be very exciting, appealing, and completely doable. Your organization needs you out on the front line, creating programs and overseeing them to their ultimate goal. Sure, running a nonprofit is more than interviewing potential employees and making a good hire. But a good hire can be critical to getting your goals and the goals of the organizations met. Each is dependent upon the other.

The workplace should be stimulating, encouraging, and a place where minds gather for the greater good. It should not feel as if it's a struggle. It should not be painful. Attracting, recruiting, and hiring personnel for your nonprofit should be something you look forward to, not something you dread. Remember, people are driving your mission. The recruiting process should be executed through open lines of communications among all parties involved. It should come from a place of strength, not fear, and it should be a well-run, adventurous, easy practice. Take heart, nonprofit leader! You are not alone. Many other executives are in the same situation and have the same challenges. Finding a long-term solution keeps you up at night because you care. Let's continue and find out how you can navigate your team through staffing challenges, while continuing to lead and assuring that your programs and services are treated as top priorities.

CHAPTER 2:

MY STORY

I have spent the last 20 years working in the nonprofit sector connecting the best people with the best causes. I began my career at a small boutique firm in New York City. Shortly after starting in a full-cycle recruiting role, it became clear to me that this is the work I'd be doing for the rest of my life. It has been my dream job, and I wouldn't do anything else. In the early days, everything about my work was exciting. I loved being part of an entrepreneurial work environment, but more importantly, knowing that my efforts benefitted the nonprofit sector was extremely gratifying. Through recruiting and staffing, I was able to impact multiple nonprofits at once, which gave me a real sense of satisfaction and fulfillment. I truly enjoyed meeting and getting to know potential candidates and hearing their work stories and aspirations. And I loved helping nonprofits identify the right candidate for their open positions.

As the conduit between the candidate and the hiring manager, I always sought to play an active role in deciding who got the job. I would give feedback to both parties about next steps and help them assess all of the information in front of them so they could be confident in their decision. I learned that when there are so many unknowns, such as the small and big time consuming tasks in the position, the direction and growth trajectory of the role, and issues to be dealt with "later," proved the hiring process to be much trickier. But when both employee and employer are transparent and clear about their intentions, the process can be seamless and lead to a long-lasting partnership.

When I founded Careers In Nonprofits in 2006, my objective was to offer an easy, efficient solution to the non-profit sector's staffing needs. I wasn't buying that a more efficient way to attract, hire, and retain professionals in the nonprofit sector couldn't be achieved. I care so much about this sector, including its growth and the important work that nonprofits do. I felt strongly that if I was going to get into the staffing game, I'd have to bring my "A

Game" and offer services and support that went beyond reviewing resumes, scheduling interviews, and extending job offers. I designed a comprehensive service package, taking on the tasks that a lot of nonprofit managers tell me they hate. The firm took on the tasks of assisting in creating or revising the job posting when needed, and ensuring that it clearly defined the role, expectations, and deliverables tied to the position. I took charge of screening candidates and developing a step-by-step interviewing and hiring process. And to close the loop, I would offer my recommendations to the hiring manager about who I believed was the perfect candidate for the job.

I acknowledge that as recruiters, the work that we do can appear very transactional, but when recruiting is handled in a transactional manner it lacks the benefits that come with doing the work as part of a team. Studies have shown that placements made utilizing a thorough process, whereby important information is gathered and shared through open lines of communications between the hiring managers and the recruiters, lead to high success rates and desirable outcomes. Understanding the role, the team dynamic, and the growth plan before you invest time and effort in recruiting, which is already time-consuming, makes the process fairly painless for hiring manager, job seeker, and recruiter, alike. This approach to serving the nonprofit sector proved to be a key differentiator, because we delved deeper to identify the qualities of the ideal candidate while adding value in the form of customer care at the same time.

The Double Whammy

As I worked with a variety of nonprofits and became intimate with their staffing woes and challenges, I gained an appreciation for the frustration that comes with an unfilled position. I would get a phone call at 5:10 p.m. on a Friday from a not-so-happy nonprofit leader who had just received a letter of resignation from a key employee. In some cases, that person had been hired less than six months ago, adding insult to injury. At other times, it would be an urgent email from a nonprofit executive director in need of a temporary employee the *very next day*. They were at Defcon Orange, one away from a full red alert, because the position had remained vacant for so long that work was piling up and the team was burnt out. I remember one client who came to us who was experiencing both at the same time, what I call the Double Whammy. On the one hand, the organization was looking for a long-term solution to its staffing crisis that would end the cycle of mis-hires; on the other, a short-term solution to deal with performance issues with the current workforce, about whom the client expressed some apprehension. The executive director had recently terminated three employees who were underperforming and had received two resignation letters in a period of four months. In this situation the client was in need of a short-term staffing solution, as well, to keep from sliding further into the abyss. This is a common case scenario in the nonprofit sector and it gives us the opportunity to partner with nonprofits and assist in significant ways. For example, by taking time to see how the position fits into the organization as a whole, and not just in the moment but three to five years down the line. Also by taking a very close look at the history of the position and what factors have contributed to other professionals being successful in it or not. Some staffing crises were less challenging than others. Some of our clients were very transparent and would share information that was pivotal to our candidate screening process and final recommendation. Having access to the full picture – including background on the job role, the reason for separation, and setting long- and short-term goals for the new hire – made a difference in our approach and, ultimately, the outcomes.

Many of the staffing problems faced by nonprofits almost always have deeper roots than what is apparent on the surface, especially those that have experienced challenges with open positions and surprise resignations over and over again. The goal of a recruiting process, whether or not a staffing firm is managing it, is to identify the best possible candidate for the open position and to do so in the easiest, most efficient way possible. But a lot of nonprofit recruiting is led from a place of scarcity and fear versus a place of strength. There's strength in knowing what is being done in and for the role and why it is being done, and a sound recruiting strategy and onboarding process can give you that.

As head of my staffing company, I look for ways to add value to the nonprofit organizations we work with and create an environment where innovative ideas can flow and best practices can be set. I've always been willing to explore, strategize, and lead a concerted effort to find solutions that are tailored to the organization. The good news is that the nonprofit sector attracts well-intentioned professionals who possess amazing skills and a servant's heart. They are looking for the right fit, too, with an organization where they can apply their individual talents in ways that align with their passion. Similarly, nonprofits are eager, in some cases desperate, to identify and onboard talented professionals who are interested in making a difference. But like dating, finding the right match isn't always easy.

As a business owner serving the nonprofit sector, I faced many of the same challenges and realizing this helped me to stifle my own fears and lean in. I know how tedious it is to have an open position for too long because you're afraid of hiring the wrong person – again. I've experienced the sinking feeling of getting two unexpected resignation letters back-to-back. There were times when we were so consumed with work that we didn't have time to recruit for ourselves. I've had to make that call to terminate an employee who was clearly a mis-hire. Others were not so clear, but staying with the company was still not an option. At some point, I realized that I needed to stop long enough to dive deeper into the situation and find the root of the cause and not just treat the symptoms. It became an obsession, not only for the benefit of my clients and the nonprofit sector but also for my sanity and the survival of my growing team.

Having to onboard and introduce a new recruiter every six months or so is mortifying. The staffing sector is notorious for having high turnover rates, but I was determined to be the exception. I spent many hours strategizing with staff members, outside consultants, relatives, and friends. I modified job descriptions and changed compensation plans. I tried adding in more flexibility in the process and also restricting flexibility. It took years of trial and error before I achieved a breakthrough that would provide a more efficient way to attract and hire staff for my clients as well as my own enterprise. Career mapping was created to turn the hiring nightmare into an employer's dream. As mentioned above, a career map is a tool that empowers nonprofit professionals to utilize their skills, experience, and unique strengths to make their mark in the world. It is a four-step process: clarity, purpose, direction, and intention.

With a career map most of the staffing challenges at my firm became easily manageable. This tool assisted with building a dynamic, cohesive, and thriving culture at Careers In Nonprofits. After seeing how effective it was, I was eager to share this process with my clients and assist them with their workforce continuity challenges. It has been an incredible journey. It didn't happen overnight but it was well worth the search. Now I'm able to teach clients and hiring managers the career mapping process to create a seamless process that they are happy to use. Most importantly, it is a process that gives them their most highly desired outcome: getting back to Job One.

Career Mapping is fun, sustainable, and proves to be a win-win approach to hiring and retaining valuable staff. I wrote this book to facilitate the connection between nonprofit employer and employee and offer a solution through career mapping that makes the hiring process manageable, practical, and effective.

CHAPTER 3:

DELIBERATE CREATION OF ROLES

O ne of the reasons nonprofits wind up recruiting for the same position over and over again, or after only five months, is because it's not enough to simply create a job description, post it in multiple places, review resumes, and interview applicants that best meet the criteria, on paper, at least. It's never been enough.

The nonprofit sector has been plagued by mis-hires and Monday morning resignations because most lack a formal process to help them avoid these hiring mistakes before the offer is extended. And, unfortunately, most job seekers are feeling the pain, too. And this, regrettably, is how bad hires happen. The job seeker is trying to fit their square peg self into a round hole, and you, as the nonprofit leader or hiring manager anxious to get back to Job One, may simply take what you can get at the time. Wouldn't it be better if the job seeker and employer took the time to sit down and co-create the role in ways that ensure both are able to meet objectives?

Because my passion lies in helping nonprofits create work environments where employees thrive and find fulfillment, I learned everything I could about how and why bad hires happen. And that's what led me to hone in on the concept of career mapping. After implementing it in my own business and seeing the benefits, I formalized it for nonprofits to help them address recruiting and retention challenges that waste time and money, and jeopardize mission fulfillment.

How does Career Mapping help?

Incorporating career mapping in your recruiting process allows you to choose the job seeker who is right for the organization and for the job seeker to know whether the position aligns with who they are and also who they want to be five years from now.

When you as an employer incorporate the creation of a career map as part of your recruiting efforts, the recruiting process becomes a beautiful journey where the employer and the employee commit to only pursuing a position that aligns with his or her ultimate career goals.

The career mapping process has four steps. These steps are designed to help you find:

- Clarity
- Purpose
- Direction
- Intention

When an employer makes career mapping part of their hiring process, they are committed to getting the hiring right from the beginning. Once the map is completed, both employer and employee are on the same page and they are moving forward in the same direction. Employers lower their risks of mis-hires and turnover rates. The employer's identification and selection of the new hire is pretty transparent and painless. There is a lot more confidence in extending the offer, preparing to onboard the new employee, and having a succinct plan of development that is a win-win for both employer and employee.

With a career map you and the new hire will find:

- More enjoyment of your 9-5
- More enjoyment of your personal time outside of work
- More satisfaction and pride in your results
- More gratifying work experiences

- More clarity, purpose, direction, and intention
- More alignment with the people you supervise or who the employee reports to
- More compensation
- More ease in accomplishing professional and personal goals
- More opportunities that you align with

How wonderful would it be if you were able to co-create the work roles with your employees? If you were to have a clear understanding of their career objectives, short- and long-term, and be an active participant in making their professional goals come to life?

The sky is the limit when it comes to the number of benefits that come from incorporating career mapping into a recruiting process. Imagine predicting when staff changes are going to happen and being prepared for it, allowing you time to plan ahead and have minimal distractions from your daily priorities. Having an active presence in your employee's career planning eliminates the guessing game and surprises. You will know ahead of time that Michael who works in Program Development is going to grad school in two years and you will have to start looking for a replacement three months before his last day, and you schedule it. Recruiting for his replacement is no longer a drag and it is scheduled into your days at the right time. The career mapping of your employees is an ongoing conversation and the goals in the plan are reviewed every 3-6 months as to become aware of bumps on the road or red flags. Red flags are to be sought after and not avoided. They are the ones that alert us that something might need our attention and protect us from blind spots. I recommend revisiting your employees' career maps during review time, and if performance reviews only happen once a year, then it should be revisited every six months at a minimum. With a career map everyone is operating from a place of strength and without fear. With a career map used as an active tool, everyone can focus on the duties that they are responsible for and enjoy and no longer spend precious time agonizing over staffing issues.

Making career mapping part of your recruiting process may require nonprofit managers to put in some additional hours on the front end, but it is time spent wisely and the ROI is worth it. You invest the time planning out the role and having a clear understanding of how to hire, who to hire and what the short term and long term goals are. It also minimizes having to recruit for the position again and again. It also pretty much eliminates "bad breakups" and employment surprises that can take you out of your happy zone of production and into a recruiting tailspin.

Using career mapping internally and co-creating my team members' goals and career dreams has been very satisfying. I have team members who have taken career mapping to heart and have created blossoming careers at Careers In Nonprofits, they have been transparent about their career goals and I have been transparent about how those career goals fit in with the company's business plan.

One of my longest standing employees shared that she wanted to take a sabbatical and it came as a surprise. This was not part of her career map the last time we revisited. However in taking every opportunity in applying career mapping to my staffing process we decided, together, that she would go on her one year sabbatical and later return to lead a brand new branch for us in a different part of the country. This fit her plan and it also fit our business plans for the near future. If I had not incorporated the elements of career mapping to this situation, I would have lost a valuable employee and she would have also lost the opportunity to continue doing work that she loved and grow in her role.

Being a conscious leader who takes into account the well-being and fulfillment of your team members makes the work that you do so much more fun and engaging. It creates an environment of trust and good vibes. This is the type of environment that attracts and retains top talent. And it allows everyone to spend time at work focusing on their Job One.

With an active career map employers enjoy high productivity and employees enjoy job security. Employers feel secure in that they have a team in which the organization, its program, and services are all well taken care of and employees feel empowered and at ease.

When a nonprofit leader empowers managers and their human resources department to use career mapping as a tool for attracting, hiring, and retention, most of the organization's hiring woes disappear. That is the power of a career mapping process that is created for every employee and that is kept alive throughout the entire working relationship. It's a simple tool. It helps with focus. It keeps everyone on the same page and it offers an edge over those nonprofits not enhancing their process with the power of a career map.

As I slowly advise our clients on using career mapping and assist them in implementing parts of it in their process I receive positive feedback on the practice. Many of the clients that I present the process to want to use more than just parts of it, they see benefits in using the entire system.

In the next few chapters we will dive deep into the process and you will learn how to co-create empowering roles with your team members. You will also learn how to achieve clarity, purpose, direction, and intention for yourself.

Armed with a sound plan to include career mapping in your process and by providing this tool to your managers you can successfully redirect the energy and focus of your team. The time gained can be used to pour into your team members and grow a strong, talented, and committed staff. Let's move into the career mapping process and see how it will help you create your dream team and get you back to focusing on your priority: Advancing your nonprofit's mission!

CHAPTER 4:

CLARITY

In attracting, selecting, and retaining the best employees for your organization it is key to have a real sense of what they really want and how/if you can meet their needs. How can you help potential or current employees get to the bottom of their true desires and share those with you? You may think that asking the question should yield the answer and then you can move on. However, it is a bit more complex than this. In order for an employee to open up to a manager they must feel that it is safe to do so. Creating a safe environment and open communication is a must when incorporating career mapping into the hiring process. Brutal honesty from the employer and employee is what makes this process magical and so effective.

Conducting a staffing process with clarity leading the way for all parties involved helps the process be carried away with ease and fewer detours and reroutes. It makes the process quicker and reduces the chances of either party being confused or making wrong turns. Clarity starts way before the interviews are scheduled and the position is posted. It starts with the creation of the position and the design of the job description. Is the open position designed with employee satisfaction, engagement, and growth in mind, along with realistic expectations from the manager? When creating a job description the duties that need to be carried forward and the experience required to carry out those duties need to be thoroughly assessed. It also helps to look at it through the lens of a job seeker. Does the combination of duties make sense? It is never good practice to throw the kitchen sink on a job description in the hopes of combining positions and finding someone who can "do it all." This way of approaching hiring has proven to fail very quickly. Taking some time to analyze and craft a succinct job description is key. Nonprofit leaders should encourage their hiring managers to update job descriptions every time the position becomes available. Nonprofit environments transform at record speed and what worked six months ago might not work today. Being cognizant of the need to have more than one person's input on the final draft of the job description is also important.

Job descriptions should:

- Be concise
- Be clear
- Include an explanation of how this position is pivotal to the overall functioning of the organization
- Focused on the position and the skills and experience required in it
- Written with the job seeker in mind
- Leave nothing to the job seeker's imagination
- Paint a detailed picture of the office environment
- Appealing and offer what's in it for the employee

When designing a job description you should not:

- Use older versions of the description
- Use terms that are unique to your nonprofit
- Only focus on listing the organization's needs
- List requirements without explaining how these fit in the whole picture
- Include vague notes that leave a lot to the imagination
- Combine positions
- Ask for more than you need in the role
- Leave important information out

The job description and the effort that is put into designing it will help you attract the right candidates to your posting. I also recommend that the position is not posted until everyone involved in the hire is 100% happy with the description. I often see how employers go to market without first ensuring that everyone involved is on the same page. Only after comparing notes – post-interviews – do they realize that they've had different expectations and have been looking for completely different people. This becomes a frustration and makes the process longer than it should be. At this point the only solution is to start from the top and design a job description that makes sense to all. Clients often come to us seeking help on a search, after having hired and recruited on their own and failing. Through diagnosing their staffing challenge we uncover that a poorly designed job description was used and the wrong hire was made. Everything matters when it comes to attracting, hiring, and retaining employees. Every step is important. The time taken on the front end to incorporate career mapping in the process is saved tenfold on the back end.

Leaders should make it a priority to gain clarity on the role and how it incorporates into the whole. It's hard to help a future employee or current employee with their clarity when we haven't gained it first. You can't lead others to where you've never been.

Helping potential employees gain clarity starts with posting the properly designed job description and guiding them through a discovery process during the interview. Oftentimes we have to create the space for applicants to determine if the position that they are applying to truly fits into their career map in both the short-term and long-term. A potential employee might look great on paper and as excited as we could be, we must slow the process down and take the time to really understand and get a sense of how clear they are about the role that they are applying to and how if fits in their 2–5 year career path.

Many candidates unconsciously morph into the job description during the interview process. We have to save them from themselves and more than that, meet them where they are. If the employer starts the process after doing the career mapping work and gaining clarity, it will become much easier to align with the right candidate and pass on those that aren't true matches to the position. It is harder to see beyond what is presented during an interview when we as employers aren't clear first on what would work and what wouldn't.

Here are some suggested interview questions to ask potential employees during the interview process:

1. What does your ideal position look like?
2. What type of office attire do you prefer?
3. What location would you ideally like your office to be in?
4. What would you like your commute to be like?
5. What type of work schedule would you like to have?
6. What are your salary expectations?
7. When would you like to get a promotion?
8. What type of manager would you like to report to?

These are excellent questions to ask as a follow up to a phone screen and prior to extending an invitation for an in-person interview or even during an interview. I particularly like to ask this after the phone screen. You might be surprised at how much information you gather that is beneficial for you to determine if a particular candidate is a strong fit for your organization and your current staffing need. If candidates fail to return the completed questionnaire in a timely manner that is very telling. Again, you are doing all that you can to weed out candidates that have the best intentions of securing a job but are not truly committed to following your recruiting process and going the extra length to stand out from the crowd. I always think that if a candidate is too busy or too confused to complete a simple questionnaire to help them determine if this position fits in their professional aspirations, then there are bigger issues to address that might surface once the candidate is onboard. We have saved ourselves from countless mis-hires by following this process. And have many examples of how skipping the clarity step has led to confusion, delayed hires, and mis-hires. This step is very important, as it is the foundation to the entire career mapping process. All the other steps flow seamlessly once we get this one right.

I'd like you to also think beyond the instances where you are conducting a search to fill a position. Career Mapping can be used as a tool to empower your existing team and offer you a more in-depth understanding of your organizational chart, taking into account everyone's career goals. Think about the difference it will make to your organization as a whole if you guided all team members through a career mapping process. Nonprofits that have incorporated career mapping into their management strategies have seen a major shift in how teams grow and transform. Career Mapping benefits the organization as a whole, making it stronger.

The practice of career mapping empowers your existing staff to take a moment and delve into their true career desires and ambitions. It's never too late to start career mapping. At Careers In Nonprofits, we have all new employees create their complete two or five year career map when they start working with us, and we encourage them to use it as a guide and update it at least once per year. Their career map is a live tool and part of an ongoing conversation. We refer to it frequently, and not only at performance reviews. Have you ever had an employee that was great on paper, was a great interviewer, but only a few months into the job it was clear that they weren't happy in the role? This is very common and if you are reading this book I'm positive that you have experienced this. In my experience the main causes of this are a poorly designed job description, a faulty interview process, and the practice of both employee and employer going into the process without clarity on their true professional desires. It's easy to fall victim to the urgency of filling a position and miss some steps, it is also very easy for applicants to get excited about a posting and accept an offer when unemployed. The key is to gain clarity and look at the big picture, being certain of how this role fits in the long-term and short-term plans of the organization and career advancement of the candidate.

We've noticed that, particularly with millennials, this tool can help them become active participants in their professional development. As you help them get in the driver's seat they gain a sense of confidence and trust. They trust that you are committed to helping them achieve their career goals and helping them navigate through the ups and downs of the work environment. I recommend that once you decide to incorporate career mapping into the fabric of your organization you do so in layers. Start with your own career mapping and then guide your direct reports through it, followed by their team members, and from there on, always incorporate it into your hiring process. It is an effective practice and my promise is that it will help you grow your organization into a vibrant, thriving, and happy workplace where team members come to advance the mission and find joy and fulfillment in their day to day activities.

It is important to have a real understanding of where your team members are. Being in the know as it concerns their desires and career plans avoids surprises. It is not common practice to help team members figure out where they would like to be as they grow their professional lives. I used to fear having those conversations. Initially, because I wasn't clear myself of my two to five year goals and later on because I feared that I was intruding on my team members' privacy, and honestly I didn't really want to know that the role that they were in did not fit their future plans if that was the case! Hear no evil, see no evil, speak no evil! Ignorance is not bliss! I learned this the hard way. After being blindsided a few times, I knew that it was more painful to not know than it was to be in the know. Therefore I took some time to gain clarity for myself and my career aspirations and company growth. As I gained clarity, I knew the type of talent I needed to carry the goals of Careers In Nonprofits forward and the type of talent that was needed to complement what I had and what the company already had in the team.

I guided this process from a place of strength, confident that little by little I would create a cohesive team that was excited to come to work every day and a team that felt empowered by their clarity, contributions and desires. I invite my team members to gain clarity and get a real understanding of what they really want in their roles and how they want to see their professional role unfold. I encourage them to sit in the driver's seat and give me the opportunity to help them make their dreams come true.

Here are some things to consider as you guide your team members and applicants through the first step of career mapping – Clarity:

1. Look around your office environment, is the environment a safe one for employees to be creative and discuss and explore tasks and duties that interest them?

2. Do employees trust their managers and co-workers?

3. Is it an open and flexible environment or rigid?

4. Can employees freely express their long-term and short-term career plans without fear?

5. During your hiring process do you incorporate assessments that help the applicant determine if this is the right job for them?

Armed with a sound job description and clarity on expectations and requirements, we can move on to the next step on the career mapping journey: Purpose.

CHAPTER 5:

PURPOSE

You have guided yourself and your team through the exercises to gain clarity about what your employees really want to do and can accomplish in the role, aligned with organizational goals. You now go on to craft a job description that is crystal clear about expectations and deliverables

Once your applicants have gained more clarity during your interview process it forces them to deal with a set of new questions: Is this position aligned with my purpose? Will I be doing what I said I wanted to do? Will my why lead me to where I want to go or will it get me off track?

Knowing with certainty why you want to do what you are planning on doing, independent of outside factors and versus what you have been doing up until now, is where it gets tricky. Why? Because it's a call to action. The questions listed at the end of the previous chapter were meant to help strip away habitual thinking and allow anyone to fearlessly pursue their true professional desires, also known as purpose.

Assessing the purpose of an open position before it is posted and interviews are conducted is crucial to continue attracting and hiring the right candidate to join your team.

As you integrate career mapping into your recruiting process and in terms of the position itself it means spending time analyzing and understanding:

- Why the position is needed
- Why the position is open
- Why the listed requirements are necessary
- Why now is the best time to recruit for this position
- Why this level of compensation

In terms of the prospective candidate, it means clearly understanding:

- Why the prospective candidate is interested in this opportunity
- Why they are a strong fit for the position
- Why are they currently on the job market
- Why your type of organization is of interest to them
- Why this is the field that they want to be in

Employers and employees that successfully navigate their career map understand the power of purpose. They use it to their advantage and they add purpose to all that they do. This makes them stand out. Defining this before you start your hiring process gives you a stronger stance. Knowing the purpose of the open position allows you to share this information with prospective employees and attract the right ones. Transparency is key, and you will be so certain of what is needed and why employees who don't align will shy away from pursuing the opportunity, and that is a good thing. You will also be able to identify quickly and clearly who makes it to the short list of potential hires.

You've sat through interviews. You know that not every professional will show up with a solid pitch that spells out what makes them a good match for the position or how their purpose aligns with the organization's mission. Helping them gain clarity and purpose, even if in the end you part ways, is so important. Investing time into potential hires offers you the privilege of only moving forward and extending offers to candidates that come with the potential to significantly contribute to the mission of your organization. And it will ensure that the position offered and accepted aligns with the employee career path in a direct way.

Long gone are the days where interviews were designed to fundamentally discuss skills and experience and assess if there was a personality fit. During the 60 to 90 minute conversation, which was mainly dominated by the employer, both employer and employee had a chance to ask some basic questions about the open position and in subtle ways, let each other know that there was an interest in continuing the conversation. A more in-depth hands-on approach is merited, as the old method has not yielded successful outcomes.

Being clear on your purpose as an employer as you start the search is pivotal and so is helping candidates get clear on their purpose during the interview process. Probing and having an open conversation might help you both determine if there is a mutually beneficial partnership. Questions that go beyond the scope of the position are important. It gives you some perspective of what the true desires of the applicant(s) are. Separating the position from the applicant for a moment during the interview also assists in understanding the applicant's career goals and if they are in alignment with your organization's needs, whether short-term or long-term.

During our clarity exercises we asked questions in an effort to understand the "what," now our questions will help us understand the "why."

1. What does your ideal position look like? Why is this important?

2. What type of office attire would you prefer? Why is this important?

3. What location would you ideally like your office to be in? Why is this important?

4. What would you like your commute to be like? Why is this important?

5. What type of work schedule would you like to have? Why is this important?

6. What are your salary expectations? Why?

7. When would you like to get your next promotion? Why is this important?

8. What type of manager would you like to report to? Why is this important?

Going through this exercise yourself first before you incorporate career mapping into your hiring process will make it easier to guide others thorough it. It should be a mandatory practice across the organization. Remember, you can't take others where you've never been. When you and your managers gain clarity and know your purpose for yourselves, you will more efficiently strategize around the talent needs of your organization. You will have a clear picture of the talent gaps and will go about adding or replacing staff with these talent gaps in mind. The idea is to onboard candidates that will complement the strengths of your existing staff, not only in theory but in true practice, so that you create a strong team without too much overlapping of skills and experience, and with all the needs and experience necessary to advance the mission of your nonprofit.

Asking the questions listed above brings to the forefront some factors that as employers we try to ignore as we desperately seek to fill our vacant positions as soon as possible. I've seen many times how avoiding spending time discussing these simple questions can lead to a mis-hire. Candidates that have not taken the time to create a compelling and unique career map to their liking might be over the moon over a job offer that seems right on the surface but that is riddled with misaligned factors. It's common to see how the excitement of an offer can immediately undermine key factors that can be deal breakers. As employers and leaders, we are responsible for shining some light on these steps and helping our employees and candidates work on the process and create their unique career maps in order to consciously and happily meet their short- and long-term career goals.

Having a clear purpose makes the going get easier when it gets tough. Challenges come up at work and having something to get us through those challenges makes a real difference. The risk of hiring a candidate that is not clear on their purpose is that they may not truly be aligned with the position. Most people think they know their purpose, but have never taken the time to truly identify it. Maybe they have adopted it from someone else, for example, wanting a particular title because that's the title that their best friend has or wanting a promotion every year because in their minds that's the only way to get ahead. Misconceptions affect the way employees show up at work and blur their judgments, so weeding through them makes it much easier to successfully create a sound career map. Their own unique map benefits them as well as you! It is our duty as hiring managers to understand the purpose behind our employees' desires and aspirations.

Now that we have clarity and purpose, let's move to direction!

CHAPTER 6:

DIRECTION

Congratulations! You are halfway through learning the process of career mapping. At this point, clarity and purpose have been established. The next step is Direction. You take pride on working on your advancement and job fulfillment. Once you have a career map in place, having clarity and knowing your purpose starts to move you in a very clear direction. The map itself becomes a tool meant to inspire and motivate you. More importantly, it's uniquely made for you and by you. As the employer, this is where your GPS kicks in. Every step builds upon the next; you can't take shortcuts. Staying on course gets you to your destination faster, with more joy, enthusiasm, excitement, and the ability to calculate risks.

Let's do a quick check-in: If, after going through their clarity exercise your candidate(s) are certain that one of their professional goals is to grow with your organization over the next five years and they have determined their intrinsic why/purpose, then the next logical step is figuring out what they need to do to get there. They have a destination; setting the course is where they should focus next. Please introduce these questions to your applicants during your interview process

1. Where have you been?
2. Where are you now in this stage of your career?
3. Where are you going?

Simple but powerful. The answers to these basic questions tell a story that they can build upon to distinguish the steps they need to get to the next level – whether they're a professional seeking career advancement and fulfillment, or aiming for expansion. For many people, getting from point A to B is a challenge. They get frustrated and start veering off course, making U-turns, wasting time, and energy. And usually, it is because they have skipped one or more of the following steps on their career map:

Take a skills inventory. This is another assessment tool I use to determine a person's strengths and the weaknesses they need to further develop to achieve their goals. A true skills assessment will paint a clear picture of what the individual brings to the table and what gaps need to be closed. At the end of this chapter, I have included a list of skills that candidates can use to rate themselves on. Now, encourage them to be honest! If they are low in the "interpersonal skills" category, they shouldn't rate themselves high to secure the position. If their management skills need improvement, their assessment should reflect that. This is for you both to have a base point from where to start your mentoring and working relationship. Being on the same page and truly aware of the candidate's talent sets expectations right from the beginning

With their skills inventory in hand, a vivid picture of what role they want to play or expand into and what their unique gifts are, they can now identify the gaps between their "now" and their "next."

Identify future goals. Being honest with themselves in terms of what the current role looks like and what they ideally would like for it to look like will help you both close the gap(s) quicker.

Create the ideal job description. What do they fantasize about when they think of the perfect role? Their future goals should be listed in their perfect role description. How does it compare to the role that they would be in. Are they very different? In theory, will they be doing the work that they are being hired to do? In practice, will they spend most of their time with hats that belong to someone else? Are their best skills being utilized? Will they be spending most of their time in their zone of genius?

The beauty of being a conscious leader and incorporating a career map in your hiring process is that you can make tweaks here and there before you burn out or before you throw in the towel. As a leader, you have the power and privilege to make significant changes, whether they are small or big, to any role and in turn make a positive impact on the organization. I truly believe and have witnessed how an empowered employee is a force for good in more ways than one!

An ideal job description enables you both to recognize what you've got and make you aware of what's missing. Those things that are missing are called future goals.

Setting the dial to SMART goals. Goals are the stepping-stone of success. So, what are SMART goals?

Where you want to be – Where you are now = SMART goals

SMART goals have been around since the 19th Century. It is still unclear who first came up with the concept. I love using SMART goals, because they provide benchmarks that are discernable and fairly easy to meet. Getting good at setting SMART goals is a pivotal part of the career mapping process. They hold you accountable and help keep you on track to your desired destination.

SMART goals are:

Specific: Not vague. Exactly what do you want?

Measurable: Goals should be quantified. How will you know if you've achieved it or not?

Attainable: Being honest with yourself about what you can reasonably accomplish at this point in your career, while taking into consideration your current responsibilities.

Realistic: It's got to be doable and practical.

Time-based: Associate a time frame with each goal. When should you complete the goal?

As you help potential hires create their career map during the interview process, they will set goals for themselves in the form of assignments and action items. They will also apply the SMART goals test to determine whether the goals they have set are as ambitious and attainable as they need to be. As they plan for growth and expansion, they will set themselves up for success by being diligent and creative, and by getting out of their comfort zone. As hiring manager your job is to determine whether their career aspirations are attainable in the role that you are offering. Being able to make the hard decision on a great candidate —for instance, turning down an overqualified candidate – comes with the territory.

That said, it's a good idea for you to use the SMART goals test to assess your motivations for hiring a candidate to make sure you are selecting the best person for the role.

For example, you're interviewing for a director's position. The minute the candidate walked in, there was a connection and an easy rapport between the two of you. You find yourself really liking this person. You'd had some concerns about skills gaps you noticed in their work experience. But they seem eager to learn.

This is a popular one. The employer hires a candidate because of their personality and ignores gaps in their skills set and level of experience. One way to avoid that as a nonprofit leader is by helping potential hires find direction. I suggest addressing the three key elements of career mapping and asking the questions during the first round of interviews. During the same interview, I'd also ask the candidate to complete the skills inventory and share the results with you. I encourage you to discuss goals and how they would meet them if hired for the position. Creating an environment whereby candidates can be transparent about their career goals during the interview will allow you, the employer, to co-create those goals. Just keep in mind the candidate should always be in the driver's seat during this process. You are the GPS that's facilitating it, helping them figure out and openly discuss with you what they want, why they want it, and where they need to go to get it allows you both to determine whether or not there is a true match between the organization's needs and the candidate's. It's simple sharing of information. The more you know, the more empowered you will be to make a good hiring decision.

Before we go any further, I want to be clear: In no way am I recommending that you take every applicant through the career mapping process before you make an offer. That would be a time drain and a logistical nightmare!

Here's what you do:

- Make a short list of applicants that look great on paper.
- Then, ask them to answer the questions laid out in the chapters dealing with clarity and purpose.
- Select the applicants with the answers that align best with the position's needs and their wants.

- During the in-person interview, work your GPS and engage them in a conversation about direction.

Not all applicants will come with 100% of the skills and experience the position requires. So for you, as the nonprofit leader, clarity also means knowing which of those things you are willing to live without. Part of their clarity is to know, with certainty, what skills they truly come with and which ones they are missing. The beauty of career mapping is that there is no right or wrong way to do this as long as everyone is fully aware and conscious of what is on the table.

I worked with a client, a well-known social service organization that was looking to hire a program development manager. The position was open due to a resignation. My client wanted to get it right this time and was eager to apply career mapping to their hiring process. I encouraged them to take their time to create a job description that was accurate, appealing, and realistic. All parties involved approved the final version of the job description, which includes in some cases the direct/indirect supervisors, human resources, and the executive director. They had clarity about areas where they were willing to be flexible and the must-haves no matter what. After posting the job description, they received 55 resumes and decided to call 18 of those. The phone screening whittled the list down to nine. Of those, eight completed the clarity questionnaire in Chapter Four, and five were invited for an in-person interview. Once they identified the two finalists, the hiring manager moved to the next phase of the career mapping process – helping each finalist achieve a real sense of how the position fit into their short-term and long-term career goals.

Both final candidates were pretty strong and neither had 100% of the requirements listed. This wasn't a challenge, because the hiring managers already were in agreement about the skills and experience they could live without. They also were not biased or influenced by the personalities of or chemistry with these candidates. They had clarity and they were able to identify what they wanted once they saw it. It made the selection process so much easier! They hired the best fit and an action plan was in place before the new hire started working.

The same approach can be taken with existing team members. It's very important to open the lines of communication with your team. They like to feel in control of their professional development. And it has been proven they are more engaged if held accountable for their own growth. We'll discuss internal staff further in Chapter Eight.

Let's move on to the next chapter: Intention.

Professional And Personal Inventory

With brutal honesty, please rate your skills and experience in the following areas on a scale of 1-5, 5 being the highest. Anything rated 3 or less is considered a weakness.

Professional Skills/Experience	Score	List 3 Ways In Which You Will Address This Weakness
Management of Small Staff		
Management of Large Staff		
Accounting/Finance		
Fundraising		
Human Resources		
Technology		
Program Development		
Personalize		
Personalize		
Related Education Required		
Other		
Personal Skills/Assets		
Ability to Focus on Task at Hand		
Ability to complete work on a Timely Manner		
Ability to Manage Difficult Situations		
Ability to Manage Work/Life Balance		
Ability to work Alone or With a Team		
Flexibility		
Self Confidence		
Health		
Personal Development		

CHAPTER 7:

INTENTION

As the leader of your nonprofit, the intentions around your role, your staff, and your outcomes must be crystal clear to you and your team.

Intention is the last piece of the puzzle that glues everything together to help you and your team members reach your professional goals. Let's first hone in on your own professional intentions and clarify them. By now, you know what you want in terms of outcomes, professional advancement, and fulfillment. You know why you want what you want, you also know where to go find it within your current role and organization, now let's figure out what to do once you get there.

In career mapping, purpose is inward and gives you meaning; intention is outward and is something you give of yourself to your organization, your team, and the world. How will you do all of this? What is the intention? In the course of action(s) that you have come up with, how you direct your steps and get to your destination is just as important as where you end up. How will you show up?

Please take some time to answer these two questions with brutal honesty:

1. What is your primary professional focus?
2. What question do you ask yourself most often based on this focus?

Determining your professional focus and your primary question will help identify what drives and motivates you. These factors may vary depending on the short-term and long-term outcomes you are pursuing. For example, as a business owner I've witnessed how my professional focus has changed over time. Most recently my focus has been on growth and innovation. Finding new ways to serve the nonprofit sector and grow my team so that we can serve even more nonprofits. The question that I ask myself most often based on my focus is, "What can I do today to innovate and grow?" Five years ago, my focus was on perfecting our recruiting process to attract and retain clients and grow our market reach. My primary question was: "How can I compete within the staffing sector?" Two years ago my focus was on expanding my business to new cities and my primary question was: "Where else in the country is our unique staffing service most needed?"

How did you answer these two questions? These answers will carve out your intentions, which in turn will give you the information you need to prepare yourself to show up with the tools needed to achieve the desired outcome for you and for your organization. And just as important, it will help you craft a job description and attract the candidates that will align with such outcomes and your organization's goals for success.

Another powerful benefit of this exercise is that it brings to focus your driving forces and any unconscious limitations you may have. If instead of asking, "What can I do today to innovate and grow?" when I was focused on growth and innovation, I would have asked, "What's stalling our growth?" I would have been focused on what's not working as opposed to focusing on what I could do "today" to innovate and grow. This way of viewing my desired outcome is much more powerful and keeps me in the space of creating and finding solutions instead of being in a frustrating and confusing place.

If after answering these questions you are not quite impressed with your answers because they are weak, ill-intentioned (it happens), or they don't serve you in a positive way. A very effective way to make them better is to change your focus and ask yourself a better question. For example, if your focus is to help your managers fill their open positions as quickly as possible and your most frequently asked question is "Why can't we get this right?" you can reframe the question by focusing on what can be improved to lower turnover and ask, "What small steps can we take and in which areas to improve our hiring process?" After taking an empowering position you might be able to clearly see that the bigger problem is not the recruiting process being lengthy or that your attention is taken away from your primary duties to focus on recruiting, the bigger problem is that your turnover rate is high, which means that you and your team are not making the right hires to begin with. Knowing this is powerful, it takes you straight to solving the main problem as opposed to just managing the symptoms.

This helps you operate from a place of strength, not weakness, because you are choosing to focus on the positive aspects of the challenge and not on what's not working. We all know how focusing on what's not working will just give us more of … what's not working! Change your perspective and your outcomes by crafting better questions for yourself and your team.

How do you incorporate this step into your recruiting process?

This step should be taken with your final candidates as you continue the career mapping conversation. Helping them define their professional intention is key to ensuring that they align with the goals of the position and the organization as a whole. The same two questions should be part of your interview questionnaire.

1. What is your primary professional focus?
2. What question do you ask yourself most often based on this focus?

Having a discussion and bringing to light their professional focus and their most frequently asked questions will give you some insights into how they will spend the majority of their working hours. I spent most of my time looking for new services or tweaking existing services to better serve our client base. If during the course of discussing this, a prospective employee confesses that their professional focus in this stage of their career is to find a job that will allow them flexibility to attend graduate school, wouldn't it be wonderful to know this ahead of time? Does this honest answer disqualify this candidate from working at your organization? It depends. It only makes a difference if you have clarity on whether flexibility can be extended in the particular role or not. Having designed an authentic job description that includes areas of flexibility would have provided you with the answer ahead of time.

You see, it is truly important to be fully prepared for the hiring process and approach it with clarity, purpose, direction, and intention. Leave nothing to chance. This preparedness is what makes some nonprofits thrive and protects them from recurring challenges like high turnover. With clear expectation, you don't have to second guess yourself in deciding if this is your best choice for a hire or not. It also gives the candidate some insights into how they think and why they do the things that they do. You are helping them build their career map in the process and this benefits you both, as you might be able to avoid making a mis-hire for your open position or help them avoid saying yes to an offer because in reality the position doesn't align with their ultimate goals. This is definitely a win-win.

The more a prospective candidate is exposed through the career mapping process the better the outcome will be. Whether an offer is extended or not, think about it as building a layer of insurance into your recruiting process, protecting you both from making time consuming and costly mistakes.

As a nonprofit leader you are constantly trying to find the ideal professional to join your team. The person who is going to dedicate all their talents, skills, and efforts to pursuing the organization's principal mission. Ideally, this person is as interested in aligning their professional identity as the organization is in aligning them to the organization's mission. This professional, in an ideal world, has the intention to grow, contribute, and succeed.

How they show up is integral to their success and contribution. Previously, we discussed the creation of the "Ideal Job Description" and how paired with the ideal candidate the selection process should be fairly straightforward and enjoyable. Helping candidates recognize their intentions for pursuing the goals listed during the direction step ensures that the motivation behind the goals aligns with their ultimate career aspirations. What is their intent for charting the course that they have chartered? In other words, what is the intention behind the SMART goals identified in Chapter Five? Part of the process is recognizing the intentions for pursuing each goal. Aside from being gainfully employed, what major contributions will prospective candidates make to best serve your organization's programs and services? As you are committed to growing and being methodical and deliberate in your professional life, living your professional life on your terms, your intentions will help align with others along your path, as well as the project and the outcomes that you are interested in pursuing.

Empowering and Disempowering Emotions

Empowering emotions fuel us. They help us maintain a healthy perspective in life. Some examples of empowering emotions are appreciation, calmness, and courage. Disempowering emotions such as anxiety, fear, and sadness hold us back and trap us in a cycle of ineffectiveness.

Oftentimes the disempowering and empowering emotions we carry around our work are born out of bad or great work-related experiences. Take some time to think of your current position or past positions and your personal experiences in them. How have they affected the way you view your work life today? How do they affect how you are crafting job descriptions and selecting your new hires?

In helping you stir up some buried memories, let's again become brutally honest as we reflect.

Please take some time to answer these questions:

1. What are your three worst work experiences?
2. What are your three best work experiences?
3. What are your five most enjoyable work tasks?
4. What are your five most avoided work tasks?

Notice how taking the time to dig deep and write your thoughts clears a lot of your thinking. Maybe it's confusing at first, which is normal, but if you stay with it, you realize that a lot of your disempowering emotions come from bad experiences and are often unresolved issues you carry with you. As you may notice from answering the questions above, you also have had positive experiences, even if you have not chosen to focus on them. Why is that? Quite simply, it's because as humans we try to avoid pain; we are conditioned to survive, and so by replaying the bad scenarios in our minds, we might think that we will avoid them. In fact, you attract them even more. Answering these questions will also help you consciously attract, hire, and retain those professionals that best align with the ultimate vision you have for your organization. Knowing where reactions or judgments come from will allow you to be an unbiased interviewer and help you identify your best hire from a place of strength and knowing.

As part of your career mapping process, you want to let go of anything that holds you down and doesn't serve you. You will find that you will make choices at every turn of your career map. These are *your* choices, not your spouse's or co-workers', yours and only yours. These choices will always be accompanied by your intentions. Don't let anyone influence your decision-making. The choice of who to hire, when, and in what role, is very important and can't be taken lightly. The clearer *you* are, the better the chances you have of making the right selection and not being confused by candidates that morph into the job description during the interview process. Once you have done the hard work of reflecting and peeling the layers to uncover who you truly are and to unveil your true Professional Identity, the rest comes easy. Your Professional Identity will be guided by your intentions and your intentions will facilitate decision-making. There will be many. Will you be true to your career map?

Please answer these questions:

1. What career choices have you made in the past that have yielded successful outcomes?

2. What career choices have you made in the past that have yielded negative outcomes?

3. If you could do it over with what you know now, what would you do differently?

4. What five new choices could you make that would improve the quality of your professional life today?

Once you change the quality of your emotions, you will make better choices. A change in your emotions can transform your professional behavior, which will in turn impact your actions. The right emotions, carried over into your career map, can take you straight to your desired outcome. Emotions like confidence, courage, and determination can add that extra mileage to your career map! Focus on better emotions, and let them create your intentions to success. The intention you set forward will make your journey speedy, productive, and successful. You will make your mark!

Incorporate these two sets of questions into your interview process. This could be a written or oral exercise given to your final candidates. These are the questions that will make a real difference, you can teach many hard skills, but emotional baggage is harder to identify and correct over time. Candidates that can answer these questions in real time or that take the time to do so after interviewing with you, have the opportunity to think about these instances and just like you did, peel back the layers and see how who they are now as professionals has been affected by past work experiences and circumstances. It gives them the chance to be an active participant in crafting their new work experience alongside you.

This final step is more a mindset than mechanical. I believe that successful employees have the right mindset first and then the right skill set. Mindset or psychology trumps mechanics any day of the week. This is why it is so important to spend the majority of the interview time and process addressing clarity, purpose, direction, and intention.

CHAPTER 8:

WHAT CAN GO WRONG?

After successfully completing your own career map, helping your team members create theirs, and incorporating it into your recruiting process, you might feel as if you have completely overhauled your organization. And you may well have! This is a great step towards ensuring that you, your team members, and new hires are all marching in the same direction and are doing so with enthusiasm and energy. Looking ahead and eager for what's to come.

Working through the four steps of career mapping – Clarity, Purpose, Direction and Intention – and empowering yourself and others with a two or five-year career map sets you apart. This is a cutting edge tool that may seem to add steps to an already cumbersome process (recruiting) but which ultimately saves you and your nonprofit time, money, and energy in significant ways. My goal is to give you back your time and help you focus on those duties that only you can do.

If your challenge is high turnover or rapid organizational growth, career mapping may be the tool you need to decrease turnover or to quickly place the right candidates in open positions. The main goal is to hire the right people the first time and to get you back to focusing on your other leadership priorities.

Over the years, I've assisted nonprofit leaders at various organizations with implementing the career mapping process. I've been welcomed with eagerness and open arms and also with resistance. Resistance by team members, management, the unknown, and of not getting it right. Fear of delving into areas that are best left untouched and fear of adding more steps to an already stressful process. Once we have successfully overcome the resistance and fear, it is easy to prove that career mapping actually makes the recruiting process much easier.

Keeping an eye on any obstacles or resistance that may come up during implementation will keep frustrations at bay and help ensure that everyone gets an opportunity to complete their unique career map in a supported environment. The dramatic changes that some of my clients have experienced in their work place after adopting career mapping are nothing short of remarkable. I've had the privilege of witnessing many positive transformations in the hiring and selection process and in the organizational growth plans of some nonprofits after career mapping has been adapted as an enhancement to their recruiting process. A memorable example is my client Benita, who is the executive director of a small social service agency and had been spending approximately 20 hours a week on recruiting efforts for her organization. Benita and her department heads were always reacting to a termination or a resignation they didn't see coming. She was continually trying to fill the same two positions—Director of Development and Receptionist, among other things. At her wits' end, Benita decided to give career mapping a chance. After completing her own, she realized she was bringing disempowering emotions to the process and changed her mindset. With career mapping, the process became streamlined and helped her effectively deal with high turnover. She hired a Director of Development and Receptionist who have been in their roles for three years and counting.

Implementing career mapping in an organization for the first time may take a concerted effort, which is a good thing. Involving everyone in the integration of this process is crucial to its effectiveness. As mentioned previously, some resistance may appear but eventually everyone will see the tremendous benefits of career mapping and will appreciate the positive workplace changes achieved through the practice.

A couple of things to always keep in mind as you start incorporating career mapping into your process:

- Allow your team members to remain in the driver's seat; they should feel in control of their professional development as well as your support. They will demonstrate more commitment, confidence, and loyalty. All these things may have already been there, but career mapping becomes the catalyst in helping them shine through and become even more visible.

- Demonstrate your interest and support in each team member's career map, and encourage active participation. This will help you create a special bond with your staff and let you spend less time strategizing around recruiting and retention and more time on projects that require your unique attention and skills.

Let's take some time to prepare for things that might present themselves as challenges when implementing career mapping into your recruiting and retention process.

One common challenge you may face is resisting the temptation to jump ahead and use career mapping in your recruiting process before completing your own unique career map. Remember, you can't take your team where you haven't been before. Completing your career map shouldn't take more that 1–2 uninterrupted hours. And you have to create space to complete it. Look at it as an important project that is the foundation of your organization's talent pool. Schedule it into your workday, and in the privacy of your office open the doors of what is possible for you and your organization. Have fun with creating your 3–5 year career plan! You are not required to share it unless you wish to, but it will be your go to map, your GPS that will keep you focused and moving forward with drive and enthusiasm. But also with minimal re-routes, confusion, and frustrations. With a clear picture of your career goals and how they align with your nonprofit's mission and vision, you are empowered to more intelligently find the missing puzzle pieces among your new staff and existing staff members. It's quite thrilling how everything makes more sense once you have concise career maps in hand that go beyond organizational charts. Nothing is left to chance, you have taken the time to plan, and in that the rewards are high.

Another challenge you might face is doubt, confusion, and resistance from your staff. They might not appreciate having a new and improved recruiting process with yet more steps in it. It might take you some time to educate them on how to roll out and incorporate career mapping in the recruiting process, but it will be time well spent. And this is yet another reason why you must complete yours first, so that the confidence of having a career map can help you communicate to your managers its benefits. You will be so empowered with clarity, purpose, direction, and intention that it will be contagious.

Be prepared to have your existing staff ask, "What about us"? They'll hear you say how career mapping has brought your career planning to the next level and will witness you utilizing career mapping in your recruiting process. They will also see new hires coming on board empowered by a career map that has your stamp of approval and they might want in on the fun! Here is when you incorporate career mapping across the board.

How do you apply this step to existing team members? The same way as described previously. The goal is to have an ongoing conversation with all team members whether at performance review time or during casual conversations. Research shows that employees are more open and less guarded to share important information when doing so in a casual environment. Active listening is key. Once you start having career mapping conversations with your teams, really listen to what they have to say. And take what they share at face value. They want to know that they are being heard and that what they think matters. Don't dismiss any piece of information that they share with you. Everything is valuable. An excellent way to empower your entire team with a career map is to conduct an organization wide workshop where everyone participates and creates their unique career map. You don't have to wait until review time to do this. It can be done as an isolated initiative to increase employee engagement, which is a hot topic these days and so vital to the well- being of a healthy organization. This workshop can be conducted by you, your human resources department, or an outside expert.

In rolling out career mapping across your organization you may find some resistance, fear, and confusion not only from those professionals being presented with it at the interview process but also by your existing team. This fear is simply fear of change, the unknown, and of being asked to take time to really think about their career as it stands in the present moment and as it evolves in the next 3–5 years. In my experience, the biggest fear faced is not knowing what they don't know! What if they don't know what they want? What if what they want won't be supported or approved by you? What if what they want they can never find within their current role? These are all legitimate questions and pretty important ones as well. The big message here that they need to hear directly from you, is that there are no right or wrong answers (particularly among existing staff), only indicators of how the co-employment relationship will evolve. For example, in my continuing career mapping discussion with current staff I've uncovered that one of my best managers may have to leave the city once her fiancé moves to another city in a year or two to finish his residency for medical school, another top manager shared that she wanted to go to Asia and take yoga classes for a year, and just recently another member I was hoping would be part of my team confessed that she might be moving to Europe with her partner within the next six months. All these revelations were news to me at each given time. Did I panic? No. These days, I rarely get a two-week notice. I do get them, but not as often. Everyone that has shared their short- or long-term plans with me have been stellar employees that have co-created their roles and that have benefitted from a career map. They are not hiding their plans and I'm not unpleasantly surprised with the news. I can and have planned around the upcoming and inevitable changes. And I embraced them. This is the same peace of mind, freedom, and power I want to give you. Once you experience it, you will not ever want to be far from a career map!

Saying all this brings me to another challenge that you may experience once you implement career mapping and that is the failure to implement. What makes career mapping work is the active use of it. Career mapping is a living, breathing tool that if kept alive and current can change the history of your organization for the better. Imagine having a dedicated staff that is committed, engaged, open, approachable, energized, and fully participating in the advancement of your nonprofit's mission. That is the dream of all leaders! Will career mapping completely eradicate your challenges as a nonprofit in the 21st century? No. Will it minimize staffing frustrations and get you back to focus on Job One? Absolutely, yes! However, you must stay true to your commitment of completely supporting the professional needs and desires of your team members. Staying highly involved in their growth and advancement will ensure that they will reciprocate that with their loyalty, smart work, and dedication. It really is a win-win. What I see some leaders do is incorporate career mapping in their recruiting and retention practices, but as time goes on the initial enthusiasm and interest fades leaving both staff members and leaders in limbo. Goals that were set in the direction phase are no longer being pursued, and six months later the needle hasn't moved much and the direction that was initially set is covered by fog. Both leaders and team members must be held responsible for keeping momentum. The career map that each individual creates should be revisited at least twice a year and ideally every quarter. Tangible goals should be listed and tracked. Team members should be held accountable for creating their future and staying true to the commitments listed in their map.

When crafting a career map the expectation is that all team members will create a plan to grow and contribute at a higher level over time. Promotions and recognition are in order. Because your team members are interested in career advancement, you would be amazed that they want to be in the know when it comes to promotions and employee recognitions. Many people wonder why getting or giving a promotion can be such a struggle. If you look closely, it is not due to a lack of effort or interest on either side. It's due to a lack of direction on both sides. Discussions around career advancement are usually mysterious and tense. Both parties may have divergent expectations. Some employers don't have a clear vision or direction of departmental growth, or have doubts about how committed an employee is. Employees may be in the dark about their employer's expansion plans or the career trajectory outlined for staff members. This is just a short list of many other possibilities that make this process hard to manage for the employer and employee. Once both parties have taken part in the career mapping process, these types of misunderstandings are cleared up.

What does it mean if a team member has missed the mark or doesn't seem to have traction with goals listed in their career map? What happens if there is little enthusiasm and the fire that once was there has dimmed? As a leader you should see these as signs that perhaps your team member has either lost clarity, doesn't have a strong enough purpose, has changed direction consciously or unconsciously, or is no longer operating from their professional identity. These are good things, they may not necessarily be red flags but what I call "aha flags"; this is the perfect time to course correct by creating new goals or steering your team member back on course.

Having open communication lines on career mapping where the goal is to only create space for your team members to succeed, and only succeed, gives you both power, freedom, peace, and the necessary tools and capacity to advance the mission of your nonprofit. This all comes with benefits to you, your team, and your nonprofit – the benefit of a thriving team environment where the work is getting done without melodrama, anxiety, or frustrations, and with the conviction that together you can change the world.

CONCLUSION

t is truly exciting to share the power of career mapping in this book with you. My wish for you is that you and your organization benefit from integrating career mapping into your recruiting process and that you are able to use less of your precious time and resources to attract, hire, and retain staff.

Career Mapping is a live tool that if used consistently helps nonprofit organizations identify the right talent at the right time, and retain and grow a cohesive team that is happy, fulfilled, and making a significant difference in the sector. The effective and frequent use of this tool lets leadership confidently manage and lead a staff that is fully engaged and dedicated. A mutual appreciation grows and trust is established in the early stages. The more stressful the recruiting process is at an organization, the more career mapping is needed and the more you may find that there is resistance when introducing this powerful tool or incorpo-rating it into your recruiting practice. Don't let this deter you from communicating the benefits and requiring that everyone in your organization use it.

Remember the four main steps:

- Clarity
- Purpose
- Direction
- Intention

Work on them one at a time and in the order listed with consistency and determination. Before you know it, your organization will be running a very smooth recruiting process. You will lower your turnover rate and will become an employer of choice in the sector.

Achieving Clarity (the What) through career mapping means that you are clear on what your role is and how to add, eliminate, or change roles in your team to support your organization's big picture. Knowing with certainty what you want to accomplish as a leader and what mile-stones you must meet to accomplish your organization's and professional goals makes identifying key players with a lot more ease and with less room for errors. No longer are you sending mixed messages to your staff on your short- or long-term goals. Everyone is on the same page. With a career map, you are confident, driven, empowered, and decisive.

On the other hand, implementing career mapping as a step in your recruiting process and as a retention tool with existing staff brings to light your team members' true professional desires and motivations. You know what's needed in each position, who can best fill the position, what requirements you are flexible on, and which ones are deal breakers. Expectations are discussed and shared openly and everyone knows what they are aiming for.

Knowing Purpose (the Why) means that you diligently have a strong, compelling reason for the decisions you make, your plan of action, and the directives you give to your team. Your Why keeps you motivated, engaged, and focused. Knowing your Why makes it easier to create a team that can align with your motives and desired outcomes. When helping applicants draw out their genuine "Whys" they and you can be certain of going into a partnership that is founded on mutual benefits that go beyond the transactional relationship of employee and employer. You win when an applicant withdraws their candidacy once they realize that the position won't satisfy their Why.

You win once you realize that as good as a candidate may seem on paper and as well as they have presented during their interview process their "Why" just won't align with your organization's purpose in the long run. Truly understanding why a potential candidate is applying to work in your organization (beyond the need of being gainfully employed) helps you create a powerful team of people that all complement each other and advance the mission of your nonprofit.

Setting Direction (the Where) means that you are certain of where you will go to find what you want and need to advance the mission of your nonprofit. Where to dedicate your focus at a given time, where to direct the effort and focus of your team. Also, knowing where your nonprofit is headed with the initiatives that you are creating and getting involved in. These are all exciting choices that you get to make once you are clear on the end goal: Your highest ideal for the nonprofit organization that you serve. Assisting applicants and team members at your organization to set a direction and know exactly where they are now, where they are going, and what goals have to be met to get from point A to point B empowers them to pursue their professional development and go all in. Having a clear direction pulls together the energy of your team and engages them at high levels

Gaining Intention (the How) is knowing how you will show up to your team, and to the community that your nonprofit serves. Are you empowered and ready to lead with the presence and leadership skills that your team and community need? Your unique career mapping will help you design your professional identity that fits well and allows you to be all you can be in your role. Crafting your leadership persona piece by piece helps you attract and retain other players that are in your league. The clearer you are in how you will go about leading and meeting your organizational goals, the easier it will be for you to see the same resolve in others. Great leaders make great teams, as long as every team member goes along for the ride and becomes a full participant. Those that have different intentions will cancel themselves out and you simply won't invite them to become part of your team with a job offer. The magic of career mapping is that it allows you to go into the employer-employee relationship with eyes wide open. With clear intentions, your potential new hires and existing staff will show up owning their professional identity and knowing how they will make the best of the opportunity given to them to make a difference. Intention adds color and flavor to the roles that each team members plays.

Once every employee is empowered with a career map, including yourself, I highly recommend revisiting the map every three to six months at a minimum, which mitigates the potential for getting lost or side tracked on the journey. It also provides an opportunity to assess the accuracy of the skills assessment and measures any progress made in skill development or goal achievement. In essence, it provides you and your team the opportunity to discover whether you are on the right track before too much time has passed.

Important questions to ask when revisiting career maps include:

- Am I still passionate?
- Am I continuing to develop new skills?
- Am I getting closer to my goals?

I invite you to be courageous, trusting, and creative in the process. Career Mapping is not a common practice yet but it is a proven tool that reduces errors in hiring and increases both engagement and retention. In a workforce era where most employees are craving empowerment and full control of their career development and at the same time crave the support of the organization's leaders, a simple process like career mapping offers both: career progression led by the employee and full support from the employer. Designed to be a win-win, career mapping is the solution that many nonprofit leaders have been desperately searching for in their attraction, hiring, and recruiting challenges.

At this point, we can agree that it is important to onboard the right people as you are trying to fill open positions. In no way should a hiring manager compromise the integrity of the team by hiring someone just because they like that person, are out of options or out of time. Empowering yourself, as the leader of the organization, and your managers to incorporate career mapping in the recruiting process will allow you to make conscious and successful hires. This practice has been a game changer for many of my clients and myself. And I'm happy and excited to share with as many nonprofits as possible.

Taking a genuine interest in the professional development, happiness, and fulfillment of your team is the secret to running a thriving nonprofit organization. Your team is looking up to you. Take the lead and get yourself in a great place first with your career map in hand! And then bring them with you; remember you can't take them where you have never been!

Happy Journey!

ACKNOWLEDGMENTS

I thank God for giving me the vision, desire, and motivation to embark on writing this second book dedicated to the leaders of the nonprofit sector and helping thousands of nonprofits advance their mission with less struggle and more joy.

I'm thankful to my family that has been ever so patient with me during the course of getting the career mapping movement in front of nonprofit leaders and professionals. My team members who are loyal and committed to spreading the benefits of career mapping, thank you.

To my friends who always cheered me on and had all the confidence that I sometimes lacked in getting this project completed, I thank you.

The opportunity to write this book was presented to me in the form of an angel coincidentally named Angela. Thanks Angela, you empowered me and helped make it possible.

To the Morgan James Publishing team: Special thanks to David Hancock, CEO & Founder for believing in me and my message. To my Author Relations Manager, Gayle West, thanks for making the process seamless and easy. Many more thanks to everyone else, but especially Jim Howard, Bethany Marshall, and Nickcole Watkins.

A heartfelt thanks to the nonprofit sector in which I have worked for most of my life and that has given me so much. Thanks for allowing Careers In Nonprofit and I the honor of being part of your missions that impact the lives of so many.

ABOUT THE AUTHOR

Nurys is a talent management and staffing expert with 20 years of experience connecting employers with talent and professionals with careers in the nonprofit sector. A native of the Dominican Republic, she began her career in executive search and recruiting in New York City. In 2006, she founded Careers In Nonprofits, now among the leading nonprofit staffing firms in the U.S.

Careers In Nonprofits serves both the employer and jobseeker market in Atlanta, Chicago, Washington, D.C. and San Francisco focusing on a range of careers from entry-level to executive positions and the ever-expanding temp-to-permanent market.

Her passion is in helping employers and employees use the power of career mapping to create a cohesive work environment and a transforming work experience.

In the summer of 2012, Nurys launched the "I Love My Job" campaign to encourage jobseekers to "really go after what they want to do," accepting only those jobs that are in line with their career goals.

She is the bestselling author of *Make Your Mark: The Smart Nonprofit Professional's Guide to Career Mapping for Success.*

Nurys resides in Northern Virginia with her husband and two young children.

THANK YOU!

Thank you for taking the time to read *Careers In Nonprofits, The Nonprofit Leader's Guide to Attracting, Hiring, and Retaining Talent*! At Careers In Nonprofits we are truly dedicated to helping nonprofits thrive and succeed with ease and passion.

We believe that making a difference in the world starts with the unity and drive of a team that shares the same outcomes and have the same standards. If you'd like to know more about how to apply career mapping to attract, hire, and retain staff, please sign up for our free master class at www.cnpstaffing.com/careermapping